T0078067

Balboa Press books may be ordered through booksellers or by contacting:

Balboa Press
A Division of Hay House
1663 Liberty Drive
Bloomington, IN 47403
www.balboapress.com
844-682-1282

Because of the dynamic nature of the Internet, any web addresses or links contained in this book may have changed since publication and may no longer be valid. The views expressed in this work are solely those of the author and do not necessarily reflect the views of the publisher, and the publisher hereby disclaims any responsibility for them.

Art by Amelia Amell.

Print information available on the last page.

ISBN: 978-1-9822-7324-8 (sc)
ISBN: 978-1-9822-7325-5 (e)

Balboa Press rev. date: 09/17/2021

TIME TRAVELERS

OF THE

DAWN

BY SHAZARA BLOOMFIELD

BALBOA.PRESS

A DIVISION OF HAY HOUSE

Preface

Time Travelers of the Dawn formed in my consciousness with piercing clarity. It began pouring in as most powerful insights do, like a roaring wave, and I myself the living experience of it tumbling to meet the shoreline.

I knew these transmissions would activate a soul remembrance within your heart and allow you an opportunity to connect with deeper aspects of your emotional body.

In you exists the light of one thousand holy suns. In you exists a well of wisdom and extraordinary potential.

May you know this now and may you be brave as you walk into the places in your heart these time travelling thoughts lead you to.

With love,

Shazara

Introduction

Do you ever look at people and feel the bittersweet journey of their soul through a glance? I do. What they have loved and also what they have lost shines through their eyes.

As an ancient soul, my heart broke early and I crumbled in a world that felt strange and unfamiliar. The density of the planet felt deeply insensitive to my spirit and because of the trauma I experienced, I was initiated into a path of healing and self-discovery early on. In time, the swells, rhythms and musings of my heart would become a guide to my future self and show me how to activate a soul remembrance in others.

These moments of complete and utter annihilation were my potent initiations. And as I turned my liabilities into assets, I discovered the diamond light within my heart and it begged for me to show others how to do the same.

I am here to remind you that deep within the heart of your suffering lies your most exquisite gifts. I am here to remind you that nothing can stand in your way when you walk in alignment with the divine.

You are a living prophecy. You are a time traveler springing forward to meet the dawn.
Keep going...

Dedication

This book of poetry is dedicated to the alchemical pain that breaks us open wider. These words are for the dreamers, the old souls, the seekers, and the visionaries. May you, beloved friend, be unafraid to travel and may you recognize that you are the inspiration for a new paradigm on Earth.

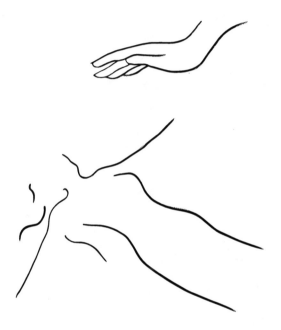

Time Travelers of the Dawn

Oh how we have traveled
through different times
and spaces
All the inner corridors
of this fleeting realm
of possibility
only to finally meet again

Oh how we have wondered
if we would ever touch
this deeply into love
and ever quench the thirst

Resting
upon the beating of our hearts
and wanting to burst
and bleed out loud
onto everything sacred
    everything beautiful
    everything safe

We have left it
in fear of the ache

and we have abandoned it all
only to know it again

This pulse

This pull

Away from heartbreak
and into benevolent faith
That love will not leave
That connection will not be severed
That peace will remain
That our truest self will not lead us astray

Love will not break us

We can pour water
onto the roots of our devotion
and watch as flowers bloom

First budding from the mud
and fighting forces to sprout
maybe resisting the sunlight
but eventually

extending out
in all directions
to breathe in the morning
and bathe in this appreciation
that nothing grows without our energy
and this

      unfolding

            is our destiny

To emerge is to be seen
and to be seen is to
truly be alive

and to be loved is to have opened
into the realms of eternity

      Unwavering
      Unquestioning
      Unrelenting in faith

In all the places
and spaces
that hold us close

and lead us away

from the losses we may never overcome

This place that forces our gripping to end

so we can fall further

into ourselves

and see in each other

what was gazing back in the mirror all along

Never alone

       Never abandoned

We stay to be seen

so we can see ourselves

more fully

so we can awaken

in the glowing light of dawn

with the knowing

that WE were the ones

we've been waiting for

Waking

Forced out of my cave
to meet you and greet you
like a river
that has been wanting
to burst open
since the beginning of time

We have been called forth
from the edges of the earth
to rest our hearts in this new space

Out of our holding
out of our hiding
out of the contraction
and into
the feeling of our own wholeness

Into the sweetness
that has been chasing us down
for all of eternity
begging
for just one moment

A taste of the nectar
that has been dripping beside you
in every breath

But you have not sipped the sweetness
you have not enjoyed the bounty

Too busy to sit
with the grace of God

Too important to soften
into the dew of the morning
and place your body
against the blades of grass
growing beneath your feet

Nowhere to be
Nothing to achieve

Only presence
Only love

Tell me
can you soften?

can you really

        really

lean in

to the only moment

you will ever know again?

Impressions

Have you asked yourself
what is the mark
you want to leave?

Because I promise
once you get clear on the answer
your whole life will change
and you will feel powerful
as this force of meaning
and purpose
ripples through you
driving everything

The call of your soul answered
the longing fulfilled

Learning the notes
to the song you had forgotten
as the sunrise came
and went
and the day turned into night again

You will understand
we are all vessels for something

Conduits carrying
   a message
   a mission
that like a wave
can ripple out
and echo into eternity

Crimson Skies

The fewer breaths we have left

the more we yearn

to take it all in

Life shows us

as it grows us

what it means to fully embrace the journey

We watch the clock slow down

as we bury those we love

and it hits us

like a massive tidal wave

We cannot postpone our greatness any longer

We cannot avoid our yearnings any more

God delivered us into form

to taste every flavor

      and see

with eyes wide open

how it feels to hold

the beating of a heart

Frozen in time
we watch it tremble
and ache
and slow down

      down

      down
with the alchemy of our presence

We are great masters
painting light against a crimson sky
falling daily
into the backdrop of the unknown
tenderly lifted again
and again
into a bittersweet symphony of devotion

A new day to paint the sky

Crystalline Grid

Lay your nameless form
upon me
and wait
while I learn to breathe again

Loving embrace
envelop me in your softness
while I wait for my heart
to beat once more

You are there
Beyond the melancholy skies
and restless hues
You wait for me
to find my feet again
and anchor
and arrive

Back into love
back into light
back into beauty

It is easy to forget
how sweet the sun feels

when you're standing in the rain

But it always returns
to lift you
from your dark days

The shine will find its way back
to greet you

You are always whole

Holding Space

Your life is going to be about holding space

Holding space for
the way your spirit
moves through this world

Holding space for
the great wisdom
in your pain and suffering

Holding space for
the softness of your joy
and how tenderly
you aim to walk through this life
in the fullness of your potential

Holding space to be deliberate
and true

Holding space for the moments
you flail about
with nothing to hold onto

For the rest of your life

you will be holding space

For grief
For loneliness
For ecstasy and bliss

May you rest
in the spaces
that feed your Wild Heart

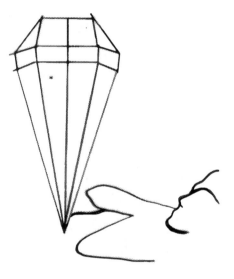

Diamond Under Pressure

Heaven on earth has found you

To tease out the jewels

from the wreckage

To polish up

these diamonds in the rough

This new world calls to you

To take the smoldering ashes of these fires

And scatter them

across the galaxy

in the shape of your signature

Heaven on earth is here now

For those with eyes to see

Under the bones

that have been buried

You are ultimately free

Free Falling

The thing about love is
you have to dive off a cliff
to get there

You have to free fall

You have to open
just enough
beyond what was previously comfortable
to really take it in

You have to
lean in
and nurture it
for the seeds to be planted
and take root within the earth

You have to know it
and grow it
from beneath your skin

What world are you in?
And are you willing to risk it all
for the sake of love?

Letting Go

You have already let go
of the things you have not lost yet
that is why you are hanging on so tightly

Everything you cherish
has slipped beyond your reach
before you have held on long enough
to squeeze the life out of every breath

Your sorrow grows
because you know
time cannot keep you from loving so deeply
and longing so madly

So you push further to know
You drive faster to grow
You drink slower
to slow
your heart beat down

To ride the moment
that has sunken into the sea of all moments

The child in you
that wandered down the road of life
is already here now

And how
How has time
taken us and shaken us so madly
How has the clock stood still
for days and months
while every last hour
passed so quickly

We are here in the frame
Stuck in between worlds
While we try
with all our might
to live like we understand
That the sands are slipping
through the hourglass
And the time has passed

To say I am sorry
      Please forgive me
      Thank you
      I love you

So do it now
If you have
some burning desire
go grant your wish

Lick your lips and taste this world
for that is all it asks of you

Before you go
unwind yourself down this path
and come to know
How honey flows
How moments glow

How time is held
in the palm of every second
you have loved

Love Has No Levels

I have seen you
standing on pillars
looking down below

and I have seen you
searching tirelessly
for pillars to stand upon

but love has no levels
it only seeks itself

Slay away the concrete falsities
from which you've clung to

Allow the walls you've built
to come crashing down

Allow the residue of the aftermath
to sweep back into the earth
from which it came

to become fertile soil once again

Remembering Home

I truly do believe
that love is the answer

And not in some
airy fairy
Pollyanna sense
But because I have felt
the presence of love

Transmute and transform
an exchange into a connection
a meeting into an awakening
an encounter into a movement
of the divine within all of us

Reaching out
to return inward

Seeking
to remember

Love carries me home when I have forgotten

Love Revisited

If you have had your heart broken
don't be angry at love

Love was
living within and around you
all along

People may hurt you
but it is love you can trust in

No matter what breaks your heart
Love will be waiting
to fill it back up again

Love is ever-present to itself

The Invitation

I have always walked upon the earth
with gentle footing
a rather deep awareness
but nothing like this devotion
I have recently grown into

Each step a question
an offering
a way to meet her more fully

As my feet land upon the earth now
I feel different
humbled
and I am listening
in ways I could never fully understand before

This earth mother
has always been my keeper
but something within me has changed
something deeper has awoken

I am taking her in
in ways I did not
have the presence for before

She has commanded me
to put my doing aside
and to simply
BE
again

And some days
I still don't understand this
within my physical body
and I resist the purity of the moment

But I know I am showing up
for our relationship
differently

With greater capacities
and more receptivity

I am tasting every nuance
and feeling her shifts

Alive
to every subtlety
that once felt like background

She is in the forefront
center stage
and I am bowing to her

As I trace my body
through her evergreen fields
I am taking my time with her

As my footprints graze
through each tiny grain of sand
I am overcome
with how she opens my heart again

We are slowing together
and in the places I may have
unknowingly forced my way through
I am asking for her understanding
I am asking for her forgiveness

In the ways I may have
pushed too hard
I am requesting she pardon me

For my lack of grace
For my lack of awareness
For my lack of love

We are learning to walk differently into the night

And we are stretching out
into the day
in new ways
softer ways
kinder ways

I am at home here now

We have less to do and more to be
her and me

And our love bursts
open
a new way of being
a new way of seeing
a new way of dreaming

This is the invitation
The Slowing Down

Deeper levels
of presence

Deeper forms
of devotion

Greater expressions of love

Mother Eternal

Sometimes I want to bow
at this great mystery
and other days
I want to rage fiercely
and then be held
against her earth
while my tears fall freely
to love her all the way through

She holds us close
in the midst of our suffering
and confusion
Mother Earth anchors us
back into her fold
to rest our weary hearts

O' Weary Traveler

Let it pass through
the chambers of your heart
so your walls
don't close in on themselves

The weight of agony
buried deep in the corners
of the earth beneath your feet

The heaviness you have learned
to tend to
through every renovation
and revision
over the course of your life

Be tender with the ache of every lost hope
with the child inside
who cannot seem to reckon
the state of this broken world

Do not let the cracks of Humanity
become you
and do not be hardened
by the pain
of the Weary Travelers among you

You are learning to ride
inside the current

Where love still can live

Inside the chaos
hearts can still be opened
and bleed into the edges of this fragile ache

So tired from trying to lift
what is not yours to carry

Let

It

Go

Into the wind
Into the light
Into the crooked corners of your heart

Let it move
outside your body

And be freed
by the space of the atmosphere

You do not have to hold it all up

Or understand
what it is
that makes its way
into the script you are writing

It is still being written

For you to read
back to yourself
when all the chips have fallen
and you are on your knees

Bleeding out into
the sea of sorrow
in your sleepless nights

Come back

You call out
begging
for the space to return

It only burns to chisel
the Diamond growing
in your heart

But why must it require
such submission

Such relentless participation
with the dark

Such deep relationship
with pain

Why must it take such exquisite loss
to emerge a Freedom Fighter
and become the wounded healer

There must be an easier way
you say
While you sit and pray
for answers

To climb down from the top
of the mountain
and still know
how to embrace the world

The Void is the Opening

You know the truth
of who you are
and yet you have forgotten

You have handed your power over
in every breath
in every movement
looking for a place to belong

The feelings you could not
spend time with
have continued to surface
and surge through you
rising up
with more and more to say

Now you can sit with them
to ask questions
and build a new way of existence

It can be painful
      Yes
to hold this much truth inside

This tide too full
for one heart's ocean

But do not part with this new life
It screams the answers
to the questions you have always asked

Here in the void
you are seen
completely
and loved still

Here you are shown
every side of your truth

Which path will you walk
which force will you align with

Do not lay down your arms
but instead Open them
to the new life that awaits

Time Standing Still

Dewdrops of remembering
who I was
before I entered this realm

How it felt
To see myself as whole
To understand the soul
that entered my body

When the world fell asleep
in the dark of the night

I was the flicker that created the light

Unveiling

In your discomfort
let the golden glow within your heart
be unearthed

As you shed the skin
that no longer
lights your soul on fire
who will you become now?

Let this frustration become purpose
Let this sorrow become service
Let this anger become action

You were chosen

Out of every star in the sky

It is you
who carries the message
It is you
who delivers the gift

Open your hands

and allow God back in

and ask yourself

how many days

and months

and even years

have I been climbing this mountain alone

We are all here

waiting

for you to return

If you can open to the gift

you will find the treasure

It may be buried very deep

but I assure you

it is there

In the shape of every prayer

In the sound of every songbird

In the color of everything

growing

within your awareness

You see
what has been veiled for so long

And you love
deeper
than you ever have before

How beautiful
that you can come back
to the places you abandoned all those years ago

To sit with the sun
To follow the curve of your own breath
To listen to the rustling wind

Have you ever really noticed
how beautiful
the world feels
when it returns to its own
still
rhythm?

Conversations With God

Hi God
I will keep coming back to you
I will keep returning to the sacred
I will keep opening my ears to hear the whispers of your
radiance

For whatever you are doing here
is terrifying
and brilliant
and heartbreaking
and necessary

And so we carry on and rest
in the blades of grass
that keep our spirits from being buried

You must not get buried
You must ache and break
and be moved by all the things
you had forgotten to love

You must let in everything
that breaks you down
so you can fill up with crystals
so you can be devoured by the light of all creation

We are here in the Colosseum

Wrestling with the beasts of every ancestor

Every silent cry we are here to answer

And so you must not surrender hope

You must not be swallowed whole

You are here to claim the divinity

that was ripped from your grandmother's hands

You are here to make this grief your opening

Unearthing Self Love

Love yourself
so deeply, so profoundly
that in your unwavering dedication
you can only attract that love

Love into the cracks
and corners and ripples and grooves
and fill them in such a way
that the fragments themselves
give birth to more radiance

Allow your brokenness
to mold you like bits of clay
unearthing the magnificence
that came from your shattered pieces

Begging you
to let that old self be buried
in the tragedies it no longer has to serve

Reading from the book of life
on this new day
and living into a world
where the dark of night

can consume all your worries

and pour a soothing balm

upon your angst

Healing and hurling

your anger

into the abyss

to be filled with drops of honey

to be soothed with sweet surrender

Where your knowing

of who you are

is enough to soothe your battle scars

Where forgiveness heals

the wounds you have carried

for too long

Where your soul's remembrance

becomes the compass

to steer your vessel

back towards the dawn

Your Ocean

I am learning not to cling
so tightly
to that which is not meant for me

Day by day
moment by moment
I am learning to lean in
to the people who care for
my highest learning and growth

I am learning not to try and win
love and validation
from those who leave me feeling
wounded and unsure of myself

I am learning it is okay
to feel lost and afraid
for tomorrow
I may awaken to a joyful heart

I am learning emotions are transient visitors
and they sometimes leave
much quicker
then I had anticipated

I am learning to trust
all that I bring into my world
even if it looks nothing
like what others are experiencing

I am learning there is always room
for love
even when, especially when
I feel exhausted and confused

I am learning my body always knows

If I tune in to how I feel
around a person or a place
there are so many hidden messages
from my own being

Trust in that
Believe in that
Rest in that

There is so much wisdom
hidden inside these cells

I am learning to come home
to the love that lives
in my core
and breathes me into life
every minute of every day

Gratitude
Gratitude
Gratitude

I am learning
there are so many ripples
in the wave of a gracious heart

How deeply
can I feel into them?

Can I become the victor
or will I choose to stay
in the small self?

Everything is happening FOR me
Nothing is happening TO me

This is the difference.

This will change EVERYTHING.

If you believe it

If you receive it

If you bow at the feet

of your challenges

they will become miracles in disguise

I promise this is true

though you may be blue

the entire ocean exists for YOU

Poem 22

The final key code of these transmissions is invisible

It exists within the fluttering of your own heart
and the way you unfold into the light of each day

It lives in the moment
                    by moment awakening
of your soul and in that which
cannot be named or described

It is how you greet the day ever-present
to meet the dance of your unique destiny

It is in this homecoming

In your remembrance of how you traveled
through time to be here now

It is how you slow dance with each breath
to find find the earth beating it's natural rhythm
within your own body

Let your Self be welcome here
Let yourself return to meet
                    the light of dawn

Art by Amelia Amell

Printed in the United States
by Baker & Taylor Publisher Services